I0015188

Arduino space race game, Bluetooth, Door Lock, Voice control etc.., projects

Arduino space race game, Bluetooth, Door Lock, Voice control etc.., projects

CONTENTS

ACKNOWLEDGMENTS

The writer might want to recognize the diligent work of the article group in assembling this book. He might likewise want to recognize the diligent work of the Raspberry Pi Foundation and the Arduino bunch for assembling items and networks that help to make the Internet of Things increasingly open to the overall population. Yahoo for the democratization of innovation!

INTRODUCTION

The Internet of Things (IOT) is a perplexing idea comprised of numerous PCs and numerous correspondence ways. Some IOT gadgets are associated with the Internet and some are most certainly not. Some IOT gadgets structure swarms that convey among themselves. Some are intended for a solitary reason, while some are increasingly universally useful PCs. This book is intended to demonstrate to you the IOT from the back to front. By structure IOT gadgets, the per user will comprehend the essential ideas and will almost certainly develop utilizing the rudiments to make his or her very own IOT applications. These included ventures will tell the per user the best way to assemble their very own IOT ventures and to develop the models appeared. The significance of Computer Security in IOT gadgets is additionally talked about and different systems for protecting the IOT from unapproved clients or programmers. The most significant takeaway from this book is in structure the tasks yourself.

1.BLUETOOTH CONTROLLED 8X8 LED MATRIX SIGN BOARD

DISPLAY USING ARDUINO

Be it the since quite a while ago extended interstates or your primary care physicians front entryway, we have sign sheets set wherever to give us data. However, these sign loads up are regularly exhausting and can't be designed according to our enthusiasm every once in a while. So in this undertaking we are gonna to manufacture a Bluetooth controlled Sign board utilizing a 8*8 Matrix show. A novel element of this task is its android application which enables the client to control all the 64 LEDs independently from the cell phone. This empowers the client to make hand crafts effortlessly and show it on the LED presentation, sounds intriguing right?!! So how about we begin...

Materials Required:

1. MAX7219
2. Arduino Pro mini
3. 8*8 LED Matrix Display
4. DC Barrel Jack
5. 20k Resistor
6. HC-05 Bluetooth Module

Circuit Diagram:

The circuit Diagram this Bluetooth controlled LED board assembled utilizing the EasyEDA application. We will utilize similar schematics to build up a PCB from it and manufacture it utilizing EasyEDA.

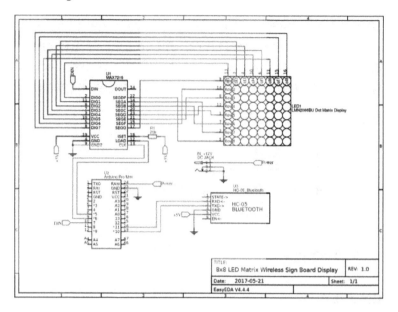

The circuit is really straight forward. The entire venture is fueled by a 12V connector, which is legitimately given to the Raw stick of the Arduino Board. This crude voltage is at that point directed to +5V which is provided to the Bluetooth module as well as the MAX7219 IC. The Tx and Rx pins of the Bluetooth module is associated with D11 and D10 of the Arduino to empower sequential association.

The advanced pins D5 to D7 is associated with the MAX7219 IC to send and get information through SPI correspondence. The ISET stick of MAX7219 is pulled high through a 20k Resistor.

For this venture I have manufactured a PCB, you can get the structure document of the PCB and utilize the equivalent or fabricate the circuit on a breadboard. Anyway because of the its unpredictability it is prescribed to either purchase a 8x8 Display module or utilize the PCB

8x8 network is valuable showcase module and can be utilized in many cool tasks:

- Controlling 8x8 LED Matrix with Raspberry Pi

- Looking over Text Display on 8x8 LED Matrix utilizing Arduino

- 8x8 LED Matrix utilizing Arduino

- 8x8 LED Matrix Interfacing with AVR Microcontroller

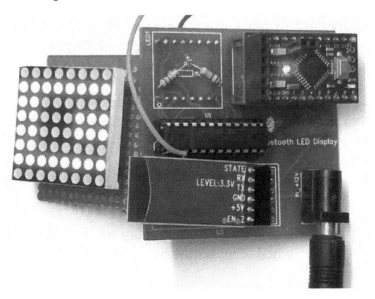

Creating the Android Application using Processing:

Before we can begin programming our Arduino, we should recognize what sort of information we will get structure the cell phone to react back to it. So how about we investigate how the Android application is made and how you can utilize it on your cell phone to control the 8x8 LED lattice.

The Android application for this undertaking was made utilizing the Processing programming. It is an Open-Source improvement application and can be effectively downloaded and put to use for creating intriguing ventures utilizing Arduino or different Microcontrollers since it can create android application and framework applications. We have effectively completed couple of tasks utilizing Processing and you can look at them by tapping on the connections underneath.

1. DIY FM Radio Using Processing

2. Computer generated Reality/Gesture control utilizing Arduino

3. Private Chat room utilizing Arduino.

4. Arduino Radar System utilizing Processing APP and Ultrasonic Sensor

5. Continuous Face Detection and Tracking utilizing Arduino

6. DIY Speedometer utilizing Arduino and Processing

7. Ping Pong Game utilizing Arduino Accelerometer

8. Biped Robot Using Arduino

9. DIY Arduino Thermal Imaging Camera

Returning to subject, it is outlandish for me clarify the total code of the android application so you would need to pick up handling independent from anyone else and after that take a gander at the code to see how it functions. Henceforth for individuals who are happy to avoid the way toward picking up Processing can download the android application from the beneath connection

- Download Android Application[APK file]

The following is the **interface of our Android Application:**

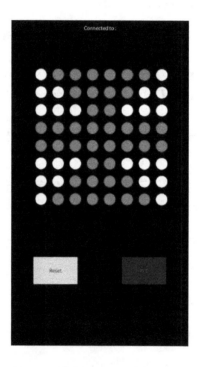

/The APK document can be straightforwardly introduced on any android application and propelled like some other application. Be that as it may, ensure your HC-05 Bluetooth gadget is named as "HC-05", in light of the fact that at exactly that point it will work.

Understanding the Processing Code:

Individuals who are intrigued to comprehend what occurs behind the screen can peruse further, other can avoid down to the following heading. Essentially the Android application associates with a Bluetooth gadget called "HC-05" during beginning up and show a lot of 64 LEDs in type of circles. At that point when the client presses the circle the circle turns red and the circle number is sent to Arduino through Bluetooth, on accepting the circle's number the Arduino turns on the LED. How about we investigate the significant lines of the Processing project to see better. The total code of the Android application can be downloaded from the beneath connection.

- Preparing Code for Android Application

We use classes and articles to show 64 LEDs with the goal that we can address every one effectively. As should be obvious in the underneath code, we utilize a for circle to emphasize from 1 to 64 utilizing an exhibit. This was each LED will have its own estimation of X position, Y position and shading and we can transform them effectively.

```
//dipslay all leds

for (int i=1; i<=64; i++)
```

```
    led_array[i].display();

    //All leds displayed

class Led{

    float X_Pos;

    float Y_Pos;

    color colour;

    //CONSTRUTOR

    Led (float tempx, float tempy, color tempc){

        X_Pos = tempx;

        Y_Pos = tempy;

        colour = tempc;

    }

    void display()

    {

        fill(colour);
```

```
    ellipse(X_Pos, Y_Pos, led_dia, led_dia);

  }

}
```

The LED's are stacked on the screen on a similar request of that of the showcase. Each LED is isolated by a separation equivalent to the width of the LED, along these lines we can without much of a stretch recognize which LED is at present chosen by the client. As appeared in the underneath program we make an exhibit where every component holds the data of the X,Y position and shade of the LED.

```
void load_leds(){

  led_array = new Led[65];

  int a=1;

  for (int j=0; j<=7; j++){

    float y = height/6 + j*(led_dia*1.5);

  for (int i=0; i<=7; i++)

  {

    float x = (width/6) + i*(led_dia*1.5); //fill(255);
```

```
//ellipse(x, y, led_dia, led_dia);

led_array[a] = new Led(x,y,color(255,255,255));

a++;

}

}

}
```

The fundamental advance in the program is to check if the client has squeezed any LED and if yes we need to change the shade of the LED and send the LED number through Bluetooth. Since now we can deliver to the area and shade of each LED effectively we can do this by simply looking at the X,Y estimations of where the client has squeezed with the X,Y estimation of the LEDs. In the event that the qualities merger into one another, at that point we change the condition of the LED and furthermore send the number through Bluetooth as demonstrated as follows.

```
//check if mouse over led //If yes send the led
number

for (int i=1; i<=64; i++)
```

```
{

  if( (mouseX < (led_array[i].X_Pos + led_dia/2))
&& (mouseX > (led_array[i].X_Pos - led_dia/2)) &&
(mouseY < (led_array[i].Y_Pos + led_dia/2)) &&
(mouseY > (led_array[i].Y_Pos - led_dia/2)))

  {led_array[i]    =    new    Led(led_array[i].X_Pos,
led_array[i].Y_Pos, led_color);

  byte[] data = {byte(i)};

  bt.broadcast(data);

  }

}
```

Aside from this, the program can likewise Reset the total LED by killing them all and furthermore you can either make a LED turn red (ON) or white (OFF) so we additionally have a switch catch for that. The switch catch is shown and sits tight for the information. Whenever squeezed the particular move will be made. The code to do the equivalent is appeared beneath as capacity which is called inside the draw circle.

```
void load_buttons()
```

```
{

  rectMode(CENTER);

  textAlign(CENTER,CENTER);

  noStroke();

  fill(#1BF2D4);

  rect(width/2-
width/4,height/1.3,width/4,height/12);    fill(0);
text("Reset",width/2-width/4,height/1.3);      //
button 1

  if (red==true)

  {                                       fill(#080F89);
rect(width/2+width/4,height/1.3,width/4,heigh
t/12);fill(255,0,0);
text("RED",width/2+width/4,height/1.3);}     //
button 2

  if (red==false)

  {fill(#080F89);
rect(width/2+width/4,height/1.3,width/4,heigh
t/12);fill(255);                                 text("
WHITE",width/2+width/4,height/1.3);} //button
2
```

```
}

void read_buttons()

{

  if (mousePressed && click_flag==true)

  {

  color_val = get(mouseX, mouseY);

  click_flag=false;

  if (color_val==-14945580)

  {

   byte[] data = {0};

   bt.broadcast(data);

   println("RESET");load_leds(); //load all led in
position and colour

  }

  if (color_val==-16248951)

  {
```

```
byte[] data = {100};

bt.broadcast(data);

if (red == true)

red = false;

else if (red == false)

red = true;

println("TOGGLE");

}

color_val=0;

}

}
```

Programming your Arduino:

The total Arduino program for this Bluetooth controlled remote Board venture is given at the base of this screen; you can utilize it legitimately and transfer it on your board. The significant lines in the program are clarified beneath.

The Bluetooth module is associated with stick 10 and

11, henceforth we need to utilize the product sequential to empower sequential correspondence on these pins and afterward we can tune in for information from these pins. We get the information got from the Bluetooth module and spare it in a variable called approaching. On the off chance that the estimation of approaching is "0" we will mood killer all the LED utilizing the code underneath

```
if (BT.available())

{

  incoming = BT.read();

  Serial.println(incoming);

  if (incoming==0)

    m.clear(); // Clears the display
```

Utilizing the benefits of approaching we require to figure out which LED the client has pushed on the cell phone and climate to kill ON or that LED. So we check if the worth is equivalent to 100. In the event that the worth is 10, at that point it implies the client has solicited to flip the shading from the LED. So we flip the variable red to know whether the LED ought to be turned on or off.

```
else if (incoming == 100)//Check if we should on
or off the LED

{

  if (red == true)

  red= false;

  else if (red == false)

  red= true;

    Serial.print("RED:"); Serial.println(red);

}
```

At long last if the worth is than 65 it implies that
the client has pushed on a LED. In light of the number
from 1 to 64 we need to figure out which LED the
client has squeezed. To flip that LED we will require
the estimation of Row and Column of that LED which
is determined and put away on factor X and Y separ-
ately and appeared on the code beneath. At last dependent on the estimation of variable red we either
turn on or mood killer the LED according to the client
demand

```
else if (incoming<=64)

   { //Calculate where to ON ro OFF the LED

     toggle=true;

   Y = incoming / 8;

   X = incoming - (Y * 8);

   if (incoming%8 == 0)

     {X = 8; Y -= 1;}

   Serial.println(X - 1);

   Serial.println(Y);

   if(red==true)

   m.setDot((X - 1), (Y), true); //LED ON

   else if (red == false)

   m.setDot((X - 1), (Y), false); //LED OFF

   }
```

Circuit and PCB Design using EasyEDA:

To structure this Bluetooth Controlled Matrix show, we have picked the online EDA device called EasyEDA. I have recently utilized EasyEDA commonly and thought that it was helpful to use since it has a decent gathering of impressions and it is open-source. In the wake of structuring the PCB, we can arrange the PCB tests by their ease . They likewise offer segment sourcing administration where they have an enormous load of electronic parts and clients can arrange their required segments alongside the PCB request.

While planning your circuits and PCBs, you can likewise make your circuit and PCB structures open so different clients can duplicate or alter them and can take profit by your work, we have additionally made our entire Circuit and PCB formats open for this circuit , check the beneath connection:

You can see any Layer (Top, Bottom, Topsilk, bottom-silk and so forth) of the PCB by choosing the layer structure the 'Layers' Window.

You can likewise see the PCB, how it will take care of creation utilizing the Photo View catch in EasyEDA:

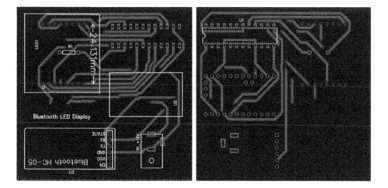

Calculating and Ordering Samples online:

Subsequent to finishing the plan of this Bluetooth Controlled Matrix PCB, you can arrange the PCB through . To arrange the PCB from JLCPCB, you need Gerber File. To download Gerber records of your PCB simply click the Fabrication Output catch in EasyEDA editorial manager page, at that point download from the EasyEDA PCB request page.

Presently go to and click on Quote Now or Buy Now catch, at that point you can choose the quantity of PCBs you need to arrange, what number of copper layers you need, the PCB thickness, copper weight, and even the PCB shading, similar to the preview demonstrated as follows:

After you have chosen the majority of the choices, click "Spare to Cart" and afterward you will be taken to the page where you can transfer your Gerber File which we have downloaded from EasyEDA. Transfer your Gerber record and snap "Spare to Cart". Lastly click on Checkout Securely to finish your request, at that point you will get your PCBs a couple of days after the fact. They are creating the PCB at exceptionally low rate which is $2. Their construct time is likewise extremely less which is 48 hours with DHL conveyance of 3-5 days, essentially you will get your

PCBs inside seven days of requesting.

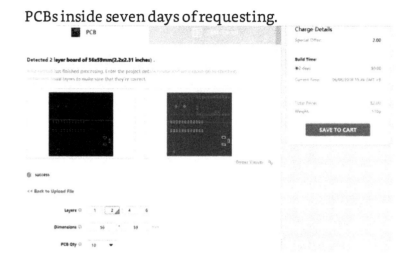

Following couple of long stretches of requesting PCB's I got the PCB tests in decent bundling as appeared in underneath pictures.

Also, in the wake of getting these pieces I have fastened all the required segments over the PCB.

In my PCB, I committed an unpolished error by choosing an inappropriate impression for the 8*8 Display module, henceforth I needed to utilize a Perf board to mount the presentation as appeared in the image. In any case, presently the impression is refreshes in the PCB and you can arrange the remedied PCB and mount the presentation module effortlessly.

Working of Bluetooth Sign board display:

When you're prepared with the Hardware either through getting the PCB or making the association on breadboard, utilize the Arduino program given toward the part of the bargain and transfer it to your Arduino Board. The android application APK record is likewise given above, use it and introduce the application on your favored Android gadget.

Power the equipment and quest for HC-05 gadget name on your telephone to combine with it. The pass key will be 1234 of course. Starting now as well as into the foreseeable future open the application that we just introduced. The application should show "associated with HC-05" at the highest point of the screen, at that point you will have the option to contact the LED on the screen and notice that a similar LED is being turned on in the board also.

You can likewise mood killer all the LED by squeezing the Reset catch and choose to kill on or a specific LED by pushing on the Toggle catch. As a matter of course which at any point LED you press will be turned on. In case you have any issue in getting it to work utilize the remarks box underneath or compose on our gatherings for increasingly specialized assistance. Expectation you comprehended the instructional exercise and delighted in structure it.

Code

```
/*
    8*8 LED Sign Board display
        library: GitHub | riyas-org/max7219  https://
github.com/riyas-org/max7219
*/
```

```
#include <MaxMatrix.h>
#include <SoftwareSerial.h>// import the serial
library
SoftwareSerial BT(10, 11); // RX, TX
int DIN = 7; // DIN pin of MAX7219 module
int CLK = 6; // CLK pin of MAX7219 module
int CS = 5; // CS pin of MAX7219 module
int maxInUse = 1;
boolean red = true;
boolean toggle = true;
MaxMatrix m(DIN, CS, CLK, maxInUse);
void setup()
{
  BT.begin(9600); //start the Bluetooth communica-
tion at 9600 baudrate
 Serial.begin(9600);
 // BT.println("Bluetooth working");
  m.init(); // MAX7219 initialization
  m.setIntensity(8); // initial led matrix intensity,
0-15
 m.clear(); // Clears the display
}
int incoming;
int Y = 0;
int X = 0;
void loop()
{
 if(BT.available())
 {
```

```
incoming = BT.read();
Serial.println(incoming);
  if(incoming==0)
  m.clear(); // Clears the display


   else if(incoming == 100)//Check if we should on or
off the LED
  {
  if(red == true)
  red= false;
  else if(red == false)
  red= true;
      Serial.print("RED:"); Serial.println(red);
  }


   else if(incoming<=64)
  {//Calculate where to ON ro OFF the LED
  toggle=true;
  Y = incoming / 8;
  X = incoming - (Y * 8);
   if(incoming%8 == 0)
  {X = 8; Y -= 1;}
   Serial.println(X - 1);
  Serial.println(Y);
  if(red==true)
  m.setDot((X - 1), (Y), true); //LED ON
  else if(red == false)
  m.setDot((X - 1), (Y), false); //LED OFF
```

Arduino space race game, Bluetooth, Door Lock, Voice control

```
    }
  }
}
```

2.ARDUINO RFID DOOR LOCK

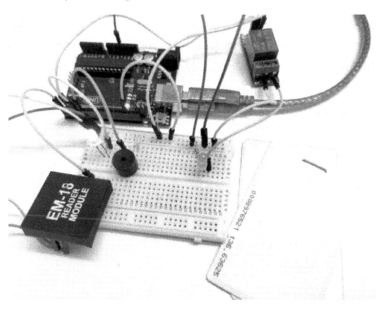

You have seen RFID entry way Lock component in certain Hotels and different spots, where you needn't bother with a key to open the room. You are given a card and you simply need to place it before a RFID Reader box, and the lock gets opened with a Beep and a Blink of LED. This RFID Door Lock can be made effectively at your home and you can introduce it in any entryway. These Door lock is simply electrically working entryway lock which gets open when you apply some voltage (commonly 12v) to it.

Here in this task we are utilizing Arduino and hand-off to trigger the Electric Door Lock and RFID to verify, so your RFID label will go about as a key. In case you spot wrong RFID card close RFID peruser a ringer will signal to caution about wrong card. In case you are new to RFID first perused its working an interfacing with Arduino.

Material Required:

- Resistors
- EM-18 Reader Module with Tags
- Arduino UNO
- LED
- Relay 5v
- Connecting wire
- Buzzer

Electric Door Lock

Arduino RFID Door Lock Circuit Diagram

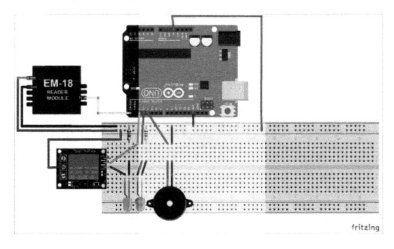

EM-18 RFID Reader:

RFID represents Radio Frequency Identification. Each RFID card has a special ID implanted in it and a RFID peruser is utilized to peruse the RFID card no. EM-18 RFID peruser works at 125 KHz and it accompanies an on-chip recieving wire and it tends to be controlled with 5V power stock. It gives sequential yield along weigand yield. The range is around 8-12cm. sequential correspondence parameters are 9600bps, 8 information bits, 1 stop bit. This remote RF Identification is utilized in numerous frameworks like

- RFID Based Attendance System,

- Security frameworks,

- Casting a ballot machines,

- E-toll street evaluating

Check all the RFID Projects here.

The yield given by EM-18 RFID peruser is in 12 digit ASCII design. Out of 12 digits initial 10 digits are card number and the last two digits are the XOR aftereffect of the card number. Last two digits are utilized for mistake checking.

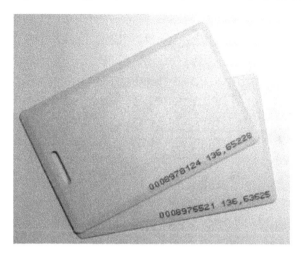

For instance, card number is 0200107D0D62 perused from the peruser then the card number on the card will be as beneath.

02 – Preamble

00107D0D = 1080589 in decimal.

62 is XOR esteem for (02 XOR 00 XOR 10 XOR 7D XOR 0D).

Consequently number on the card is 0001080589

Code and Explanation:

The total RFID Door Lock Arduino Code is given toward the part of the bargain.

In the underneath code, the RFID label number are put away in the "burn tag". "180088F889E1" is my RFID label number put away in the microchip of the Transponder. The duration of the label number is 12 we have characterized the cluster like "scorch input [12]", 12 characterizes the no. of character or size of exhibit.

```
char tag[] ="180088F889E1";

char input[12];

int count = 0;

boolean flag = 0;
```

For discover the tag no. of your Arduino you can allude this article.

Presently, in beneath code, we arrangement the pins of the Arduino UNO board for the activity and the serial.begin() is utilized for the sequential information transmission. Here the stick 2 is utilized for the handoff activity, stick 3 is for the reserve red LED and stick 4 is for the bell.

```
void setup()
```

```
{

  pinMode(2,OUTPUT);

  pinMode(3,OUTPUT);

  pinMode(4,OUTPUT);

  Serial.begin(9600);

}
```

The restrictive body of the code is void circle() , for the reserve red LED the stick 3 stays HIGH until any assignment performed.

We will check if there is any sequential information accessible utilizing the if condition. Means we will check if there is any RFID tag is getting examined. In the event that any sequential information (RFID Tag no.) is coming we will spare it in input[] cluster which we characterized for sparing RFID label number.

```
  void loop(

{

  digitalWrite(3,1);
```

```
if(Serial.available())

{

  count = 0;

  while(Serial.available() && count < 12)

  {

    input[count] = Serial.read();

    count++;

    delay(5);

  }
```

Presently we will think about the examined RFID card no. with the number which we have characterized in roast tag[] exhibit. In the event that both the umber matches, at that point we set the banner variable to 1 and on the off chance that an inappropriate card is checked or both the numbers don't coordinate, at that point we set the banner variable to 0.

```
if(count == 12)

  {
```

```
count =0;

flag = 1;

while(count<12 && flag !=0)

{

  if(tag[count]==input[count])

  flag = 1;

  else

  flag= 0;

}
```

On the off chance that you spot right RFID tag, the banner gets equivalent to 1, for this situation the stick 2 goes HIGH (through which a hand-off worked) and the stick 3 goes low as of now, after postponement of 5 sec the two pins will come back to its underlying condition. Hand-off will be additionally associated with Electric Door Lock, so with the hand-off turned on, the Door Lock will be opened, and following 5 seconds it will again get bolted.

```
if(flag == 1)
```

```
{

  digitalWrite(2,HIGH);

  digitalWrite(3,LOW);

  delay(5000);

  digitalWrite(2,LOW);

}
```

In the event that you place an inappropriate RFID card, the banner will be zero and the bell start signaling cautioning that the RFID card isn't right.

```
if(flag == 0)

  {

    for(int k =0; k<= 10; k++)

    {

      digitalWrite(4,HIGH);

      delay(300);

      digitalWrite(4,LOW);
```

```
    delay(300);

    }

    }
```

Working of Arduino Based RFID Door Lock

The RFID framework comprises of two segments: a RFID tag and a Reader. The RFID label comprise of co-ordinated circuit and a recieving wire, incorporated circuit is for the capacity of the information, and a radio wire is for transmitting the information to the RFID Reader module. At whatever point the RFID label comes in the scope of RFID peruser, RF sign power the tag and after that label starts transmitting information sequentially. Information is additionally gotten by the RFID peruser and the peruser sends it to the Arduino board. What's more, after that according to the code in smaller scale controller distinctive assignment performs.

In our circuit, we have officially spared the estimation of RFID tag in the code. In this way, at whatever point that specific label comes in range, the hand-off gets actuated. Here we have associated a LED with Relay to illustrate, yet this LED can be supplanted by an Electric Door Lock, so that at whatever point the Relay gets initiated the lock will be opened.

On the off chance that we filter some other RFID card, the ringer will begin signaling as it's an inappropriate RFID tag. Consequently, for the entryway lock framework we have utilized this idea that the entryway will just get opened by utilizing the privilege RFID tag. The hand-off will itself get deactivated following 5 seconds, the entryway will be shut following 5 seconds, and you can change this postponement in the code.

Complete code is given underneath.

Code

```
char tag[] ="180088F889E1";
char input[12];
int count = 0;
boolean flag = 0;
void setup()
{
```

```
 pinMode(2,OUTPUT);
 pinMode(3, OUTPUT);
 pinMode(4, OUTPUT);
 Serial.begin(9600);
}
  void loop()
{
 digitalWrite(3,1);
 if(Serial.available())
 {
  count = 0;
 while(Serial.available() && count < 12)
  {
   input[count] = Serial.read();
   count++;
   delay(5);
  }
  if(count == 12)
  {
   count =0;
   flag = 1;
   while(count<12 && flag!=0)
   {
    if(tag[count]==input[count])
    flag = 1;
    else
    flag= 0;
}
  if(flag == 1)
  {
   digitalWrite(2,HIGH);
```

```
   digitalWrite(3,LOW);
  delay(5000);
  digitalWrite(2,LOW);
 }
 if(flag == 0)
 {
  for(int k =0; k<= 10; k++)
 {
  digitalWrite(4,HIGH);
 }
 }
 }
 }
 }
```

3.AUTO INTENSITY CONTROL OF POWER LED USING ARDUINO

"Be a brilliant flash, lights off till it's dull!" in some cases we neglect to mood killer the lights and waste power and you should have likewise observed road light turned on in the day. We have officially constructed few circuits on Dark locator where lights mood killer naturally in the event that it is splendid outside and turns on the off chance that it is dull outside. In any case, this time, in this circuit we are not just turning On and off lights dependent on light conditions yet additionally fluctuating the force of light as indicated by outside light conditions. Here we have utilized LDR and PWM idea with Arduino for diminishing or expanding the brilliance of the 1 watt Power LED consequently.

Essentially, PWM alludes to Pulse Width Modulation, the yield signal through a PWM stick will be a simple sign and gained as a computerized sign from the Arduino. It utilizes the obligation cycle of the computerized wave to create the consecutive simple incentive for the sign. Furthermore, that sign is additionally used to control the splendor of the Power LED.

Material Required

- LDR
- Arduino UNO
- Capacitor (0.1uF)
- Resistor (510, 100k ohm)
- 1 watt Power LED
- Transistor 2N2222
- Breadboard
- Connecting wires

Circuit Diagram

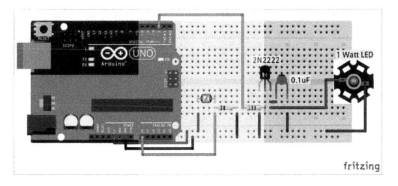

Code and Explanation

The total Arduino code for Automatic LED dimmer is

given toward the end.

In the underneath code, we are characterizing the PWM stick and the factors to be utilized in the code.

```
int pwmPin = 2; // assigns pin 12 to variable pwm

int LDR = A0; // assigns analog input A0 to vari-
able pot

int c1 = 0;  // declares variable c1

int c2 = 0;  // declares variable c2
```

Presently, on the up and up, we are first perusing the worth utilizing the direction "analogRead(LDR)" at that point spare the simple contribution to a variable named "esteem". By doing some mathematic computation we are producing the PWM signal. Here, we are controlling the power of light utilizing PWM just if the simple worth is under 500, and in the event that it is in excess of 500 we totally mood killer the lights.

```
int value = analogRead(LDR);

  Serial.println(value);

  c1 = value;
```

```
c2= 500-c1;   // subtracts c2 from 1000 ans saves
the result in c1

if (value < 500)

{

digitalWrite(pwmPin, HIGH);

delayMicroseconds(c2);

digitalWrite(pwmPin, LOW);

delayMicroseconds(c1);

}

if (value > 500)

{

  digitalWrite(2,LOW);

}

}
```

You can study PWM in Arduino from here.

How it Controls the Light Intensity Automatically:

According to the circuit graph, we have made a voltage divider circuit utilizing LDR and 100k resistor. The voltage divider yield is feed to the simple stick of the Arduino. The simple Pin detects the voltage and gives some simple incentive to Arduino. The simple worth changes as indicated by the opposition of LDR. Along these lines, if is dull over the LDR, its opposition get expanded and henceforth the voltage esteem (simple worth) diminishes. Consequently, the simple worth change the PWM yield or the obligation cycle, and obligation cycle is further corresponding to force of light of intensity LED. So the light over the LDR will naturally control the force of Power LED. The following is the stream chart how this will function, upside bolt sign is designating "expanding" and drawback bolt sign is specifying "diminishing".

Force of light (on LDR) ? - Resistance? - Voltage at simple pin? - Duty cycle (PWM)? - Brightness of Power LED ?

On the off chance that its full splendid outside (when simple worth builds more than 500) the power LED turns off.
This is the means by which you can control the force of light consequently utilizing LDR.

Further check our everything the LDR related circuits here.

Code

```
int pwmPin = 2; // assigns pin 12 to variable pwm
int pot = A0; // assigns analog input A0 to variable pot
int c1 = 0;  // declares variable c1
int c2 = 0;  // declares variable c2
void setup() // setup loop
{
 pinMode(pwmPin, OUTPUT);
 pinMode(pot, INPUT);
 Serial.begin(9600);
}
void loop()
{
  int value = analogRead(pot);
 Serial.println(value);
 c1 = value;
 c2 = 500-c1;      // subtracts c2 from 1000 ans saves
the result in c1


 if(value < 500)
 {
digitalWrite(pwmPin, HIGH);
delayMicroseconds(c2);
digitalWrite(pwmPin, LOW);
delayMicroseconds(c1);
 }
 if(value > 500)
 {
 digitalWrite(2,LOW);
 }
```

Anbazhagan K

}

4.VOICE CONTROLLED LEDS USING ARDUINO AND BLUETOOTH

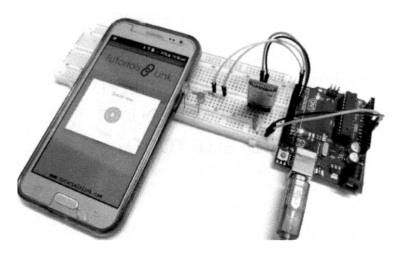

Controlling LEDs with voice order is by all accounts a troublesome assignment, yet it's simple and you can rapidly fabricate it. We simply need an Arduino UNO to sequentially speak with HC-06 Bluetooth module and a cell phone to send voice order to Bluetooth module HC-06. For accepting voice direction we are utilizing "Arduino Bluetooth Voice Controller" android application which you can installed from play store (connect is given underneath).

Material Required

- Associating wires

- HC-06 Bluetooth Module

- Arduino UNO

- Resistor 220 ohm (2 nos.)

- LEDs (Red, and Green)

- Breadboard

- Arduino Bluetooth Voice Controller (Installed from play store)

HC-06 Bluetooth Module:

Bluetooth can work in the accompanying two modes:

- Order Mode

- Working Mode

In Command Mode we will have the option to arrange the Bluetooth properties like the name of the Bluetooth signal, its secret word, the working baud rate and so forth. The Operating Mode is the one wherein we will have the option to send as well as get information between the PIC Microcontroller and the Bluetooth module. Thus in this instructional exercise we will toy just with the Operating Mode. The Command mode will be left to the default settings. The Device name will be HC-05 (I am utilizing HC-06) and the secret key will be 0000 or 1234 and in particular the default baud rate for all Bluetooth modules will be 9600.

The module takes a shot at 5V supply and the sign pins work on 3.3V, consequently a 3.3V controller is available in the module itself. Consequently we need not stress over it. Out of the six sticks just four will be utilized in the Operating mode. The stick association table is demonstrated as follows

S.No	Pin on HC-05/ HC-06	Pin name on MCU	Pin number in PIC
1	Vcc	Vdd	31st pin
2	Vcc	Gnd	32nd pin
3	Tx	RC6/Tx/CK	25th pin
4	Rx	RC7/Rx/DT	26th pin
5	State	NC	NC
6	EN (Enable)	NC	NC

Check our different undertakings to become familiar with Bluetooth module HC-05 with different microcontrollers:

- Bluetooth Controlled Toy Car utilizing Arduino

- Bluetooth Controlled Home Automation System utilizing 8051

- Voice Controlled Lights utilizing Raspberry Pi

- PDA Controlled FM Radio utilizing Arduino

and Processing

- Interfacing Bluetooth Module HC-06 with PIC Microcontroller

- Bluetooth Controlled Servo Motor utilizing Arduino

Circuit Diagram

Circuit chart for this Voice Controlled Lights is given underneath, while transferring the code in the Arduino UNO disengage the Rx and Tx sticks and associate again after the code is transferred.

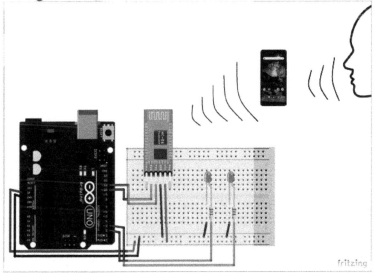

Code and Explanation

The total Arduino code for Voice controlled LEDs is

given toward the end. Here we are clarifying couple of parts of code.

Here, in the underneath code we are characterizing the pins for Rx and Tx.

```
int TxD = 11;

int RxD = 10;
```

Presently, set stick second and third of the Arduino as yield.

```
pinMode(2, OUTPUT);

pinMode(3, OUTPUT);
```

In void circle work, Arduino will check the approaching qualities constantly and controls the LEDs according to the voice direction. Arduino will kill on or the LED by the given Voice order. We are sparing all the gotten direction in factor "Worth"
On the off chance that the worth is "altogether LED turn on" at that point both the LEDs turns ON, similar to this we have coded other voice directions for killing on or the individual LED.

```
if (bluetooth.available())

  {

   value = bluetooth.readString();

   if (value == "all LED turn on"){

   digitalWrite(2, HIGH);

   digitalWrite(3, HIGH);

    }

   if (value == "all LED turn off"){

    digitalWrite(2, LOW);

    digitalWrite(3, LOW);

    }

   if (value == "turn on Red LED"){

   digitalWrite(2, HIGH);

    }
```

```
if (value == "turn on green LED"){

  digitalWrite(3, HIGH);

  }

if (value == "turn off red LED"){

digitalWrite(2, LOW);

  }

if (value == "turn off green LED"){

  digitalWrite(3, LOW);

  }

}
```

Working Procedure:

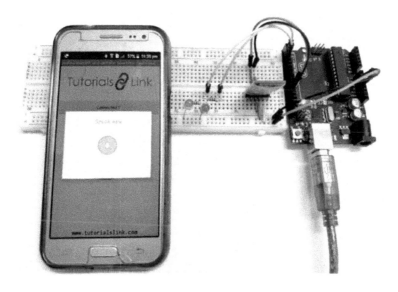

Stage 1:- Connect all parts according to the circuit chart; disengage Rx as well as Tx pins while transferring the code.

Stage 2:- Download the application called "Arduino Bluetooth Voice Controller" is free on play store.

Stage 3:- Open the application and pursue the picture beneath, similar to initially tap on "associate with Bluetooth gadget" and select your Bluetooth module and check on the off chance that it is associated or not. At that point click on the mic symbol to talk and send the voice direction to the HC-06 module.

www.tutorialslink.com

Note: when you are associating your Bluetooth module just because with your cell phone it will request the password, utilize 0000 or 1234.

Stage 4:- After setting up every one of the things, you simply need to send the voice order by utilizing the application which is additionally sent to Bluetooth module HC-06 and the HC-06 sequentially speak with the Arduino UNO and after that the errand is executed according to the direction. The beneath demonstrates the order and the activity to be performed by the direction:

S. No.	Command	Action

1.	all LED turn on	Both Red and Green LED turns ON
2.	all LED turn off	Both Red and Green LED turns OFF
3.	turn on Red LED	Red LED turns ON
4.	turn on green LED	Green LED turns ON
5.	turn off red LED	Red LED turns OFF
6.	turn off green LED	Green LED turns OFF

Likewise, check Voice Controlled LED with Raspberry and Bluetooth.

Code

```
#include <SoftwareSerial.h>
String value;
int TxD = 11;
int RxD = 10;
int servoposition;
SoftwareSerial bluetooth(TxD, RxD);
void setup() {
 pinMode(2, OUTPUT);
 pinMode(3, OUTPUT);
 Serial.begin(9600);    // start serial communication
at 9600bps
```

```
 bluetooth.begin(9600);
}
void loop(){
 Serial.println(value);
 if(bluetooth.available())
  {
  value = bluetooth.readString();
   if(value == "all LED turn on"){
  digitalWrite(2, HIGH);
  digitalWrite(3, HIGH);
   }

   if(value == "all LED turn off"){
   digitalWrite(2, LOW);
   digitalWrite(3, LOW);
   }

   if(value == "turn on Red LED"){
  digitalWrite(2, HIGH);
   }

   if(value == "turn on green LED"){
   digitalWrite(3, HIGH);
   }


   if(value == "turn off red LED"){
  digitalWrite(2, LOW);
   }
   if(value == "turn off green LED"){
   digitalWrite(3, LOW);
   }
 }
```

Arduino space race game, Bluetooth, Door Lock, Voice control

}

5.ARDUINO COLOR MIXING LAMP USING RGB LED AND LDR

Imagine a scenario in which we can produce various hues utilizing a solitary RGB drove and make our room's corner progressively appealing. In this way, here is a basic Arduino based shading blending light which can change shading when there is change in light in the room. So this light will consequently will changes its shading as per the light conditions in the room.

Each shading is the mix of Red, Green as well as Blue shading. So we can create any shading by utilizing red, green as well as blue hues .So, here we will fluctuate PWM for example power of light on LDRs. That will further changes the force of red, green as well as blue shading in RGB LED, and various hues will be deliv-

73

ered.

Underneath table demonstrates the shading mixes with particular change in obligation cycles.

Materials required:

- 3 x hued strips (red, green, blue)

- 3 x 1-kilohm resistors

- 1 x Breadboard

- 3 x LDRs

- 1 x Arduino UNO

- Jumper wires

- 3 x 220-ohm resistors

- 1 x RGB LED

LDR:

We will utilize photoresistor (or light-subordinate resistor, LDR, or photograph conductive cell) here in this circuit. LDRs are produced using semiconductor materials to empower them to have their light-delicate properties. These LDRs or PHOTO RESISTORS takes a shot at the rule of "Photograph Conductivity". Presently what this standard says is, at whatever point light falls on the outside of the LDR (for this

situation) the conductance of the component incre-
ments or at the end of the day, the obstruction of the
LDR falls when the light falls on the outside of the
LDR. This property of the lessening in opposition for
the LDR is accomplished in light of the fact that it is a
property of semiconductor material utilized superfi-
cially.

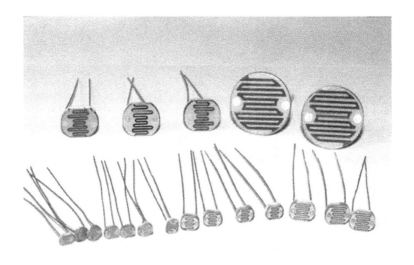

Here three LDR sensors are utilized to control the
splendor of individual Red, Green as well as Blue LED
inside RGB Led. Study controlling LDR with Arduino
here.

RGB LED:

There are 2 kinds of RGB LEDs, one is basic cathode
type (basic negative) and other is basic anode type

(regular positive) type. In CC (Common Cathode or Common Negative), there will be three positive terminals every terminal speaking to a shading and one negative terminal speaking to each of the three hues.

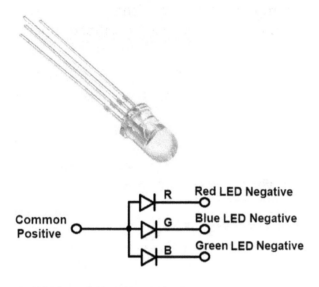

Common Anode RGB LED

In our circuit we are going to utilize CA (Common Anode or Common Positive) type. In Common Anode type, in the event that we need RED LED to be ON in, we have to ground the RED LED stick and power the regular positive. The equivalent goes for every one of the LEDs. Learn here to interface RGB LED with Arduino.

Circuit Diagram:

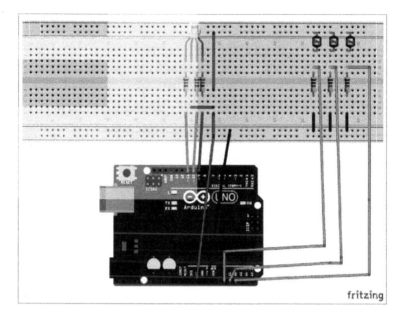

The total circuit graph of this task is given above. The +5V and ground association appeared in the circuit outline can be acquired from the 5V and ground stick of the Arduino. The Arduino itself can be fueled from your workstation or through the DC jack utilizing a 12V connector or 9V battery.

We will utilize PWM to change splendor of RGB drove. You can become familiar with PWM here. Here are some PWM models with Arduino:

- Variable Power Supply By Arduino Uno

- DC Motor Control utilizing Arduino

- Arduino Based Tone Generator

Programming Explanation:

Initially, we proclaim every one of the information sources and yield sticks as demonstrated as follows.

```
const byte red_sensor_pin = A0;

const byte green_sensor_pin = A1;

const byte blue_sensor_pin = A2;

const byte green_led_pin = 9;

const byte blue_led_pin = 10;

const byte red_led_pin = 11;
```

Pronounce beginning estimations of sensors and leds as 0.

```
unsigned int red_led_value    = 0;

unsigned int blue_led_value   = 0;

unsigned int green_led_value  = 0;

unsigned int red_sensor_value = 0;
```

```
unsigned int blue_sensor_value = 0;

unsigned int green_sensor_value = 0;

void setup() {

    pinMode(red_led_pin,OUTPUT);

    pinMode(blue_led_pin,OUTPUT);

    pinMode(green_led_pin,OUTPUT);

    Serial.begin(9600);

}
```

In circle segment, we will take yield of three sensors with analogRead(); capacity and store in three unique factors.

```
void loop() {

    red_sensor_value    =    analogRead(red_sen-
sor_pin);

    delay(50);

    blue_sensor_value    =    analogRead(blue_sen-
sor_pin);
```

```
delay(50);

green_sensor_value = analogRead(green_sen-
sor_pin);
```

Print those qualities onto the sequential screen for troubleshooting reason

```
Serial.println("Raw Sensor Values:");

    Serial.print("\t Red: ");

    Serial.print(red_sensor_value);

    Serial.print("\t Blue: ");

    Serial.print(blue_sensor_value);

    Serial.print("\t Green: ");

    Serial.println(green_sensor_value);
```

We will get 0-1023 qualities from the sensors yet our Arduino PWM pins have 0-255 qualities as yield. So we need to change over our crude qualities to 0-255. For that we need to separate crude qualities by 4 OR essentially we can utilize mapping capacity of Arduino to change over these qualities.

```
 red_led_value  = red_sensor_value / 4;  // define
Red LED

 blue_led_value  = blue_sensor_value / 4;  // de-
fine Blue LED

 green_led_value = green_sensor_value / 4; // de-
fine Green Led
```

Print mapped qualities to sequential screen

```
Serial.println("Mapped Sensor Values:");

 Serial.print("\t Red: ");

 Serial.print(red_led_value);

 Serial.print("\t Blue: ");

 Serial.print(blue_led_value);

 Serial.print("\t Green: ");

 Serial.println(green_led_value);
```

Use analogWrite() to set yield for RGB LED

```
analogWrite(red_led_pin,red_led_value);  // indi-
cate red LED

 analogWrite(blue_led_pin,blue_led_value);    //
indicate blue LED

 analogWrite(green_led_pin,green_led_value); //
indicate green
```

Working of Arduino Color Mixing Lamp:

As we are utilizing three LDR's thus, when light epi-
sode on these sensors ,it's opposition changes accord-

ingly voltages additionally changes at simple pins of Arduino which is going about as an information pins for sensors.

At the point when force of light changes on these sensors, it's separate drove in RGB will gleam with measure of opposition changing and we have distinctive shading blending in RGB drove utilizing PWM.

Code

```
const byte red_sensor_pin = A0;
const byte green_sensor_pin = A1;
const byte blue_sensor_pin = A2;
const byte green_led_pin = 9;
const byte blue_led_pin = 10;
const byte red_led_pin = 11;
unsigned int red_led_value    = 0;
unsigned int blue_led_value   = 0;
unsigned int green_led_value  = 0;
unsigned int red_sensor_value  = 0;
unsigned int blue_sensor_value = 0;
unsigned int green_sensor_value = 0;
void setup() {
  pinMode(red_led_pin,OUTPUT);
  pinMode(blue_led_pin,OUTPUT);
  pinMode(green_led_pin,OUTPUT);
  Serial.begin(9600);
}
void loop() {
  red_sensor_value = analogRead(red_sensor_pin);
```

```
  delay(50);
  blue_sensor_value = analogRead(blue_sensor_pin);
  delay(50);
      green_sensor_value  =  analogRead(green_sen-
sor_pin);
  // print those values onto the serial monitor
  Serial.println("Raw Sensor Values:");
  Serial.print("\t Red: ");
  Serial.print(red_sensor_value);
  Serial.print("\t Blue: ");
  Serial.print(blue_sensor_value);
  Serial.print("\t Green: ");
  Serial.println(green_sensor_value);
  // convert from 0-1023 to 0-255
  red_led_value  = red_sensor_value / 4;  // define Red
LED
   blue_led_value  = blue_sensor_value / 4;  // define
Blue LED
  green_led_value = green_sensor_value / 4; // define
Green LEd
  // print mapped values to serial monitor
  Serial.println("Mapped Sensor Values:");
  Serial.print("\t Red: ");
  Serial.print(red_led_value);
  Serial.print("\t Blue: ");
  Serial.print(blue_led_value);
  Serial.print("\t Green: ");
  Serial.println(green_led_value);
  // use analogWrite() to set output for RGB LED
   analogWrite(red_led_pin,red_led_value);  // indi-
cate red LED
```

```
  analogWrite(blue_led_pin,blue_led_value); //indi-
cate blue LED
  analogWrite(green_led_pin,green_led_value); //in-
dicate green
}
```

6.SPACE RACE GAME USING ARDUINO AND NOKIA 5110 GRAPHICAL DISPLAY

Programming has a ton of fun and it just showed signs of improvement with advancement stages like Arduino. Pretty much every developer around here would have attempted to build up some sort of game utilizing the language that they picking up/rehearsing. This encourages them to tune their programming abilities in a fun yet gainful manner. I have been a major fanatic of Arduino as far back as I got acquainted with it and constantly needed to take a stab at something cool with it, when I discovered how cool it can get with a Graphical LCD like Nokia 5110 alongside Arduino my concept of building up a game kicked in. It was a fascinating method to adjust few programming aptitudes and have a ton of fun simultaneously, so however you all may be keen on building up your game too. Subsequently In this instructional exercise we will figure out how we can make Decent Game utilizing Arduino and Graphical LCDs.

We have officially manufactured that good old Snake game utilizing Arduino so this time we are having a go at something new and we named this game as Space Race Game where you have to guard your ship from foe boats utilizing joystick.

Game Plan:

Before we start up, it is essential to plan out how you game would really function. I went with the Nokia5110 Graphical LCD and Joystick for my equipment choice. I expect in this instructional exercise that you have additionally chosen the equivalent. Since the Nokia 5110 doesn't accompany a ton of room we have plan our whole game inside the 84*48 pixel goals of our presentation. We have effectively made instructional exercises on the best way to interface Nokia 5110 LCD with Arduino and Joystick with Arduino.

Inside this space we need to firmly fit in the gaming

region and the score board territory which will show things like score and stuff. It is critical to know the pixel area of where you spot stuff to monitor the pixel areas and update them on the screen.

When the game screen appearance is chosen we need to choose the characters in our game. For my game we have just two, the player character which is a space transport and a foe character which should sort of resemble an outsider spaceship. The Nokia LCD can show bitmap pictures, so I chose to utilize that alternative to show my space dispatch and the foes.

So we will have a space deliver that is dashing through the outsiders spaceships, this spaceship will have three paths to changes so as to stay away from a hit with the outsiders. At unsurpassed the outsiders can involve just two track and the player ought to have the option to pass through the free track. When these thoughts are closed we can continue with the Hardware and after that the programming.

Circuit Diagram:

The circuit for this Arduino game is exceptionally basic; we simply need to interface the Nokia 5110 LCD module and the Joystick with Arduino. The total circuit chart is demonstrated as follows

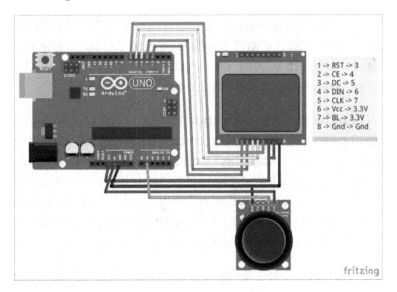

The Nokia 5110 LCD works with the 3.3V and the Joystick module work child 5V, so ensure you interface the LCD with 3.3V just, on the grounds that 5V may harm it for all time. The LCD speaks with Arduino through SPI convention and the Joystick just read ADC to peruse the adjustment in voltage. The association set-up will look something like this underneath

Pre-requisites:

Before we plunge into the programming part it is significant for you individuals to be helpful with the Display module and the Joystick, so you can utilize the accompanying instructional exercises to find out about them and after that get back here to ensure things are working the manner in which we need it to!

- Nokia 5110 LCD Interfacing with Arduino

- Joystick module interfacing with Arduino

Programming Arduino for Space Race Game:

The total program for the game can be found toward the part of the bargain; you can utilize it legitimately on your Arduino IDE and transfer it to you Board. Be that as it may, on the off chance that you need to recognize what really occurs inside the code, at that point read further.

As consistently we start our program with including our library header records, we need three libraries for this undertaking out of which the SPI library is added to your IDE of course. The other two library must be downloaded from the Adafruit Github page. Pursue the LCD interfacing instructional exercise referenced in the pre-imperatives area on the off chance that you don't know how to include the library.

```
#include <SPI.h> //SPI librarey for Communication

#include <Adafruit_GFX.h> //Graphics lib for LCD

#include <Adafruit_PCD8544.h> //Nokia 5110 LCD library
```

In case you have pursued the instructional exercise you should realize that it is conceivable to show the bitmap pictures in the LCD. So we need to change over the picture required into bitmap code by utilizing programming referenced in the instructional exercise, you can choose any picture from the web and use it by changing over them to bitmap code. Ensure the picture is basic enough to be shown on our LCD screen, check the review before really taking a stab at the LCD screen. In our program we have utilized two bitmap characters one is the space dispatch and the other is the foe send, the bitmap code for both is included our code as demonstrated as follows.

```
//Bitmap Data for SpaceShip

static const unsigned char PROGMEM ship[] =

{

B00000000,B00000000,

B00000001,B00000000,

B00000011,B10000000,

B00000010,B10000000,

B00000010,B11000000,

B00000111,B11000000,

B00001101,B11100000,

B00011111,B11110000,

B00111111,B11111000,
```

```
B01111111,B11111100,

B01111111,B11111100,

B01111111,B11111100,

B00011111,B11110000,

B00000111,B11100000,

B00000000,B00000000,

};

//Bitmap Data for enemyship

static const unsigned char PROGMEM enemy[] =

{

B00000101,B11000000,

B00001011,B11100000,

B00000011,B11100000,

B00110011,B11111000,

B01111111,B11111100,
```

```
B10111111,B11111010,

B01110111,B11011100,

B01111110,B11111100,

B00111111,B11111100,

B11101111,B11101110,

B11000001,B00000110,

B10000001,B00000010,

B10000000,B00000010,

B00000000,B00000000,

};
```

We need to indicate the pins to which the Nokia LCD 5110 presentation is associated with. The presentation is spoken with utilizing the SPI correspondence, in case you have pursued the circuit chart over, the code to initialise the LCD will be as per the following you need not transform it.

```
Adafruit_PCD8544        display      =      Ada-
fruit_PCD8544(7, 6, 5, 4, 3); //Specifiy the pins to
```

which the LCD is connected

Inside the arrangement work we simply start the Serial screen at 9600 baud rate with the goal that we can troubleshoot stuff and afterward introduce the LCD show. We likewise need to set the differentiation of the LCD show, each show will work the best in an alternate complexity level, so play with the incentive to check which suits the best for you. At long last we additionally clear the showcase screen to begin new.

```
void setup() {

  Serial.begin(9600); //Serial Monitor for Debugging

  display.begin(); //Begin the LCD communication

  display.setContrast(30); //Set the contrast of the display

  display.clearDisplay();   // clears the screen and start new

}
```

When the screen is cleared we bounce into the circle work and there we show the game screen. The game screen is only which shows a fundamental skeleton for the game alongside the score and speed level. We have utilized the line capacity to draw three lines as outskirts and to the correct we show the content score and speed simply like the old retro hand held gaming gadgets.

```
void gamescreen()

{

//Draw the Border for Screen

  display.drawLine(0, 0, 0, 47, BLACK);

  display.drawLine(50, 0, 50, 47, BLACK);

  display.drawLine(0, 47, 50, 47, BLACK);

//Enter Default Texts

  display.setTextSize(1);

  display.setTextColor(BLACK);

  display.setCursor(52,2);

  display.println("Speed");

  display.setCursor(54,12);
```

```
display.println(game_speed);

display.setCursor(52,25);

display.println("Score");

display.setCursor(54,35);

display.println(score);

}
```

Next we need to get the contribution from client to permit him/her to control the space dispatch. The info will be gotten from the Joystick module which is associated with stick A1. The simple incentive from the sensor will be 512 in the event that it isn't moved and will increment and reduction when moved along the X-pivot. We utilize these qualities to decide whether the client needs to move to left or to one side. You should peruse the Joystick interfacing with Arduino instructional exercise referenced in the pre-necessities in case you thinking that its difficult to comprehend the beneath program.

```
//Get input from user

Joy_X = analogRead(A1); //Read the X vaue from
Joystick
```

```
if (Joy_X < 312 && POS!=1 && control==true) //If
joy stick moves right

{ POS--; control = false;} //Decrement position of
spaceship

else if (Joy_X > 712 && POS!=3 && control==
true) //If joy stick moves right

{ POS++; control = false;} //Increment position of
spaceship

else if (Joy_X >502 && Joy_X<522) //If joystick
back to initial position

control = true; //Preare it for next move

//Input from user received
```

Subsequent to getting the situation of the spaceship from the client we need to put the space send at that specific spot. We utilize the underneath capacity and pass the estimation of situation as a parameter, at that point dependent on the position the space ship is put in its separate track.

```
void player_car(char pos) //Place the spaceship
based on the user selected position

{
```

```
if (pos==1)

display.drawBitmap(2, 32, ship, 15, 15, BLACK);

if (pos==2)

display.drawBitmap(18, 32, ship, 15, 15, BLACK);

if (pos==3)

display.drawBitmap(34, 32, ship, 15, 15, BLACK);

}
```

Since our spaceship is put on the screen and is prepared for dashing we need to present the adversary ships who will contend alongside the player. Each time a foe ship has crossed the screen we accept he is dead and when he is dead we need to make another space transport. The beneath capacity does notwithstanding. It makes another situation for two adversary ships and places them on the highest point of the screen.

```
if (enemy_dead) //Check of enemy ships are dead

  { //If they are dead

  enemy_0_pos = POS; //create first enemy above
```

```
  the space ship

  enemy_1_pos = random(0,4); //create secound
enemy at some other random place

  enemy_phase = 0; //Bring the enemy form the top

  enemy_dead = false; //Enemy is created so they
are not dead anymore

  }
```

In the wake of putting the adversary dispatches on the highest point of the screen we need to cut it down with the goal that it skewers as though our player is dashing upwards, to do that we simply have to increase the stage (where the picture is shown) so it descends gradually. The equivalent is accomplished for both the foe dispatches as demonstrated as follows

```
enemy_ship          (enemy_0_pos,enemy_phase);
enemy_phase++; //Place the first enemy on screen
and drive him down

  enemy_ship          (enemy_1_pos,enemy_phase);
enemy_phase++; //Place the secound enemy on
screen and drive him down
```

The capacity enemy_ship is demonstrated as follows,

it is fundamentally the same as the player vehicle work however here we have two parameters. One is for setting the adversary on a track as well as the other is for moving the foe towards the base.

```
void enemy_ship(int place, int phase) //Place the
enemy_ship in the new place and phase

{

  if (place==1)

  display.drawBitmap(2, phase, enemy, 15, 15,
BLACK);

  if (place==2)

  display.drawBitmap(18, phase, enemy, 15, 15,
BLACK);

  if (place==3)

  display.drawBitmap(34, phase, enemy, 15, 15,
BLACK);

}
```

The following bit of code should check if the space ship has maintained a strategic distance from the adversary transport. To check this we have to know the situation of adversary ships and the player's space deliver. Since we know all that we simply need to check if the space ship position is as same as the foe transport. We check this just if the adversary ship has come to close to the space deliver. In case the player has not maintained a strategic distance from the adversary it means game over.

```
if (enemy_phase>22 && ((enemy_0_pos == POS)
|| (enemy_1_pos == POS)) ) //If the Spaceship
touches any one of the enemy

 game_over(); //Display game over
```

In the event that the player has maintained a strategic distance from the foe effectively, at that point we should execute the foe and give the player a point. To do this we simply check if the adversary has come to the base of the screen and in the event that it does we murder it utilizing the code beneath

```
if (enemy_phase>40) //If thespace ship escapes
the enemies

 {enemy_dead = true; score++;} //Increase the
score and kill the enemies
```

Anbazhagan K

What fun it would be, on the off chance that we don't build the trouble of the game as we get high scores. So we utilize another capacity which at that point screens the score of the player and dependent on the score it will expand the speed of the game. The speed is really constrained by utilizing the postpone work this will control the revive interim of the game in this way making it quick or moderate.

```
void   Level_Controller() //Increase the speed of
game based on the score.

{

  if (score>=0 && score<=10) //If score 0-10

  {

    game_speed = 0; delay(80); //slow the game by
80ms

  }

  if (score>10 && score<=20) //If score 10-40

  {

    game_speed = 1; delay(70); //slow the game by
70ms
```

```
}

  if (score>20 && score<=30) //If score 20-40

  {

   game_speed = 2; delay(60); //slow the game by
60ms

  }

  if (score>30 && score<=40) //If score 30-40

  {

   game_speed = 3; delay(50); //slow the game by
50ms

  }

}
```

Arduino Space Racer Game working:

In the wake of ensuring the equipment and program is seen, simply construct the circuit and transfer the code to the Arduino Board. You should see the game beginning as demonstrated as follows

Utilize the joystick to get away from the foe transport by moving left or right. For staying away from every foe you will get your score expanded by one. At the point when the score goes high the speed of the game will likewise build, the speed increment by 10ms for each ten points you score. You can feel free to expand upon this game to present new levels or each make some equipment changes to control it however movement utilizing an accelerometer. Imagination is as far as possible. For your reference you figure out how to utilize Accelerometer with Arduino here.

Expectation you comprehended the undertaking and appreciated structure it. By any chance you have confronted any issue in getting this to work, kindly don't hesitate to post the issue on the remark area underneath or utilize the gatherings for specialized assistance. Glad gaming!!

Check the total code beneath.

Code

```
/* SPACE RACE Game using Arduino and Nokia 5110
LCD
 * Input -> Joystick (A0,A1)
*/
#include <SPI.h> //SPI librarey for Communication
#include <Adafruit_GFX.h> //Graphics lib for LCD
#include <Adafruit_PCD8544.h> //Nokia 5110 LCD
librarey
//More info on how to interface Nokia 5110 with LCD
//Bitmap Data for SpaceShip
static const unsigned char PROGMEM ship[] =
{
B00000000,B00000000,
B00000001,B00000000,
B00000011,B10000000,
B00000010,B10000000,
B00000010,B11000000,
B00000111,B11000000,
B00001101,B11100000,
B00011111,B11110000,
B00111111,B11111000,
B01111111,B11111100,
B01111111,B11111100,
B01111111,B11111100,
B00011111,B11110000,
B00000111,B11100000,
```

```
B00000000,B00000000,
};
//Bitmap Data for enemy ship
static const unsigned char PROGMEM enemy[] =
{
B00000101,B11000000,
B00001011,B11100000,
B00000011,B11100000,
B00110011,B11111000,
B01111111,B11111100,
B10111111,B11111010,
B01110111,B11011100,
B01111110,B11111100,
B00111111,B11111100,
B11101111,B11101110,
B11000001,B00000110,
B10000001,B00000010,
B10000000,B00000010,
B00000000,B00000000,
};
Adafruit_PCD8544 display = Adafruit_PCD8544(7, 6,
5, 4, 3); //Specifiy the pins to which the LCD is con-
nected
int enemy_0_pos, enemy_1_pos, enemy_phase;
int Joy_X;
int game_speed = 0;
int score = 0;
char POS=2;
boolean enemy_dead = true;
boolean control = true;
```

```
void setup() {
 Serial.begin(9600); //Serial Monitor for Debugging
  display.begin(); //Begin the LCD communication
  display.setContrast(30); //Set the contrast of the display
  display.clearDisplay();  // clears the screen and start new
}
void loop() {
  display.clearDisplay();  // clears the screen and start new

  gamescreen(); //Displays the box, score and speed values

  //Get input from user
 Joy_X = analogRead(A1); //Read the X vaue from Joystick
 if (Joy_X < 312 && POS!=1 && control==true) //If joy stick moves right
  { POS--; control = false;} //Decrement position of spaceship
  else if (Joy_X > 712 && POS!=3 && control==true) //If joy stick moves right
  { POS++; control = false;} //Increment position of spaceship
  else if (Joy_X >502 && Joy_X<522) //If joystick back to initial position
  control = true; //Preare it for next move
  //Input from user received

  player_car(POS); //Place the Space ship based on the
```

input from user

```
 if(enemy_dead) //Check of enemy ships are dead
 { //If they are dead
 enemy_0_pos = POS; //create first enemy above the
space ship
    enemy_1_pos = random(0,4); //create secound
enemy at some other random place
 enemy_phase = 0; //Bring the enemy form the top
 enemy_dead = false; //Enemy is created so they are
not dead anymore
 }
 enemy_ship          (enemy_0_pos,enemy_phase);
enemy_phase++; //Place the first enemy on screen
and drive him down
        enemy_ship    (enemy_1_pos,enemy_phase);
enemy_phase++; //Place the secound enemy on
screen and drive him down
 if (enemy_phase>22 && ((enemy_0_pos == POS) ||
(enemy_1_pos == POS)) ) //If the Spaceship touches
any one of the enemy
 game_over(); //Display game over


 if (enemy_phase>40) //If thespace ship escapes the
enemys
 {enemy_dead = true; score++;} //Increase the score
and kill the enemys
 Level_Controller(); //BAsed on score increase the
speed of game
```

```
  display.display();  //Update the display with all the
changes made so far
}
void  Level_Controller() //Increase the speed of game
based on the score.
{
 if(score>=0 && score<=10) //If score 0-10
 {
  game_speed = 0; delay(80); //slow the game by 80ms
 }
  if(score>10 && score<=20) //If score 10-40
  {
  game_speed = 1; delay(70); //slow the game by 70ms
 }
  if(score>20 && score<=30) //If score 20-40
  {
  game_speed = 2; delay(60); //slow the game by 60ms
 }
  if(score>30 && score<=40) //If score 30-40
  {
  game_speed = 3; delay(50); //slow the game by 50ms
 }
}
void enemy_ship(int place, int phase) //Place the
enemy_ship in the new place and phase
{
 if(place==1)
    display.drawBitmap(2,  phase,  enemy,  15,  15,
```

```
BLACK);
  if(place==2)
    display.drawBitmap(18, phase, enemy, 15, 15,
BLACK);
  if(place==3)
    display.drawBitmap(34, phase, enemy, 15, 15,
BLACK);
}
void game_over() //Display game over screen
{
 while(1) //The program will be stuck here for ever
 {
  delay(100);
 display.clearDisplay();
 display.setCursor(20,2);
 display.println("GAME OVER");


  display.display();
 }
}
void gamescreen()
{
//Draw the Border for Screen
 display.drawLine(0, 0, 0, 47, BLACK);
 display.drawLine(50, 0, 50, 47, BLACK);
 display.drawLine(0, 47, 50, 47, BLACK);
//Enter Default Texts
 display.setTextSize(1);
 display.setTextColor(BLACK);
```

```
 display.setCursor(52,2);
 display.println("Speed");
 display.setCursor(54,12);
 display.println(game_speed);
 display.setCursor(52,25);
 display.println("Score");
 display.setCursor(54,35);
 display.println(score);
}
void player_car(char pos) //Place the spaceship based
on the user selected position
{
 if(pos==1)
 display.drawBitmap(2, 32, ship, 15, 15, BLACK);
  if(pos==2)
 display.drawBitmap(18, 32, ship, 15, 15, BLACK);
  if(pos==3)
 display.drawBitmap(34, 32, ship, 15, 15, BLACK);
}
```

7.INTERFACING TILT SENSOR WITH ARDUINO

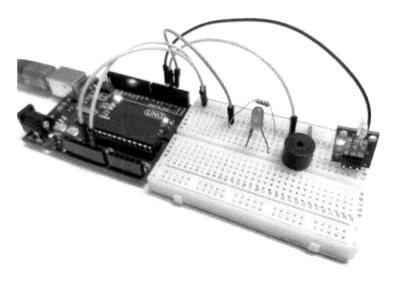

A Tilt Sensor switch is an electronic gadget that recognizes the direction of an article and gives its yield High or Low in like manner. Essentially, it has a mercury ball inside it which moves and makes the circuit. So tilt sensor can kill on or the circuit dependent on the direction.

In this undertaking, we are interfacing Mercury switch/Tilt sensor with Arduino UNO. We are controlling a LED and ringer as indicated by the yield of the tilt sensor. At whatever point we tilt the sensor the alert will be turned on. You can likewise observe the working of tilt sensor in this tilt sensor circuit.

Material Required

- Mercury Switch/ Tilt Sensor
- Arduino UNO

- Buzzer
- Resistor - 220 ohm
- Breadboard
- Connecting wires
- LED

Circuit Diagram

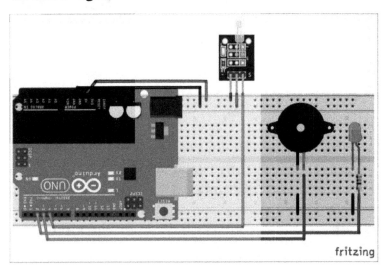

fritzing

To associate a Tilt sensor with the Arduino, it requires 5v dc contribution to work. That 5v is provided utilizing Arduino UNO and the yield of Tilt sensor is taken at PIN 4 of the Arduino. Driven is associated with the PIN 2 of the Arduino UNO with 220-ohm resistor to constrain the current to a protected worth. Also, the ringer is straightforwardly associated with the PIN 3 of the Arduino UNO.

Tilt Sensor

It is a mercury switch based tilt sensor module which gives high at its yield stick when tilted it needs a 5v of dc input. It's a three-terminal gadget comprise of info, ground, and yield. It has a glass cylinder comprise of two terminal and fluid mercury ball. The fluid mercury ball closes and opens the circuit when slanted a specific way. The working and interior structure of the module is given beneath:

Internal Structure

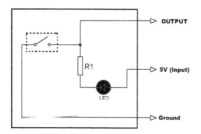

Working of Tilt Sensor

CASE 1: NOT TILTED

At first, when it is in NOT tilted situation as appeared in the picture underneath, it gives LOW yield due to the fluid mercury complete the circuit by associating the two terminals. At the point when the yield is LOW ready LED stay ON.

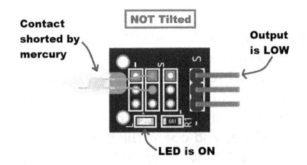

CASE 1: TILTED

When it is slanted a specific way or edge, the fluid mercury breaks the contact between the metal anodes and the circuit gets open. Thus, we get HIGH yield in this condition and the locally available LED turns off.

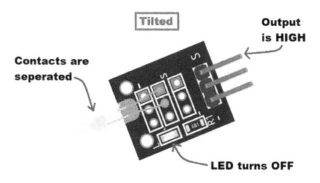

Code and Working Explanation

The total Arduino code for Interfacing Tilt Sensor with Arduino is given toward the end.

In the underneath code, we are characterizing the pins as Input and Output. Stick 2 and Pin 3 are set as yield pins for LED and Buzzer individually and Pin 4 is set as contribution to get input information from the Tilt sensor.

```
void setup() {

  pinMode(2, OUTPUT);

  pinMode(3, OUTPUT);

  pinMode(4, INPUT);

}
```

Presently, at whatever point the Tilt sensor is slanted past a specific edge the Output of tilt sensor gets HIGH. This yield is perused Pin 4. In this way, at whatever point the Pin 4 is HIGH, it turns ON the LED and Buzzer.

```
void loop() {

 if (digitalRead(4) == 1)

 {

 digitalWrite(2, HIGH);

 digitalWrite(3, HIGH);

 delay(300);

 digitalWrite(2, LOW);

 digitalWrite(3, LOW);

 delay(300);

 }

}
```

This can be cool side interest undertakings like an

antitheft box, alert box or mystery report box.

Code

```
void setup() {
 pinMode(2, OUTPUT);
 pinMode(3, OUTPUT);
 pinMode(4, INPUT);
}
void loop() {
 if (digitalRead(4) == 1)
 {
 digitalWrite(2, HIGH);
 digitalWrite(3, HIGH);
 delay(300);
 digitalWrite(2, LOW);
 digitalWrite(3, LOW);
 delay(300);
 }
}
```

8.BLUETOOTH CONTROLLED SERVO MOTOR USING ARDUINO

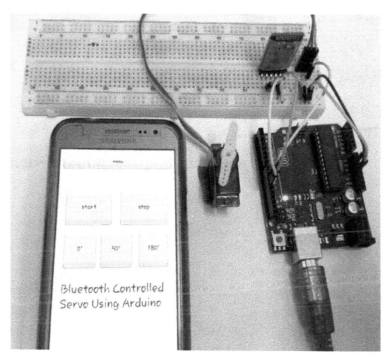

Bluetooth Controlled Servo Using Arduino

Utilizing a Servo engine is basic in Robotics for exact control. Here, in this instructional exercise we are demonstrating how to utilize a Servo engine remotely with an Arduino UNO as well as an Android gadget by means of Bluetooth association. We officially controlled servo with Arduino, this time we are controlling Servo remotely utilizing Bluetooth Module HC-06.

Material Required

- Arduino UNO
- HC-05 or HC-06 Bluetooth module

- Servo Motor
- Roboremo App from Playstore
- Breadboard
- Connecting wire

HC-06 Bluetooth Module

Bluetooth can work in the accompanying two modes:

- Direction Mode

- Working Mode

In Command Mode we will have the option to design the Bluetooth properties like the name of the Bluetooth signal, its secret key, the working baud rate and so forth. In Operating Mode we will have the option to send and get information among the PIC Microcontroller as well as the Bluetooth module. Subsequently in this instructional exercise we will toy just with the Operating Mode. The Command mode will be left to the default settings. The Device name will be HC-05 (I am utilizing HC-06) and the secret word will be 0000 or 1234 and above all the default baud rate for all Bluetooth modules will be 9600.

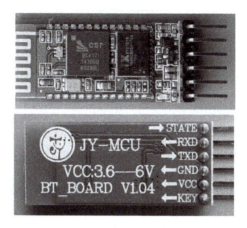

The module chips away at 5V supply and the sign pins work on 3.3V, consequently a 3.3V controller is available in the module itself. Henceforth we need not stress over it. Out of the six sticks just four will be utilized in the Operating mode. The stick association table is demonstrated as follows

S.No	Pin on HC-05/ HC-06	Pin name on MCU	Pin number in PIC
1	Vcc	Vdd	31st pin
2	Vcc	Gnd	32nd pin
3	Tx	RC6/Tx/CK	25th pin
4	Rx	RC7/Rx/DT	26th pin
5	State	NC	NC

6	EN (Enable)	NC	NC

Check our different undertakings to get familiar with Bluetooth module HC-05 with different microcontrollers:

- Bluetooth Controlled Toy Car utilizing Arduino

- Bluetooth Controlled Home Automation System utilizing 8051

- Voice Controlled Lights utilizing Raspberry Pi

- Advanced cell Controlled FM Radio utilizing Arduino and Processing

- Interfacing Bluetooth Module HC-06 with PIC Microcontroller

Circuit Diagram

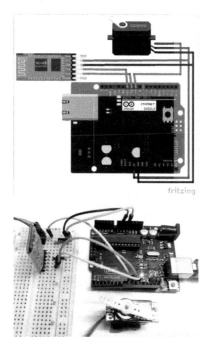

Configuring Roboremo App for Controlling Servo:

Stage 1:- Download the Roboremo application from the Android Play Store and introduce it in your cell phone. In case of introducing it you will see the application window as appeared in the figure1 and by tapping on 'Menu' catch you will see window appeared in figure2 underneath:

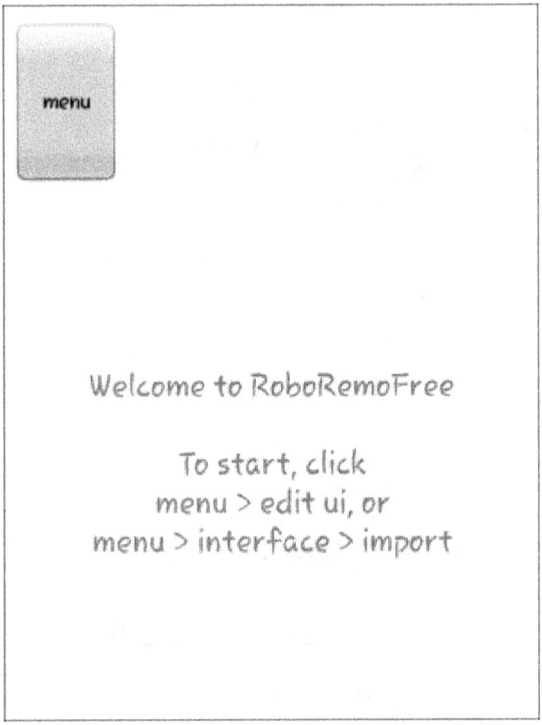
menu
Welcome to RoboRemoFree
To start, click
menu > edit ui, or
menu > interface > import

Figure1

Figure2

Stage 2:- Then click on associate catch and you will see the window appeared in figure3 beneath then you need to choose 'Bluetooth RFCOMM' and after that you will have the option to interface your HC-06 bluetooth module with your android application 'Roboremo'.

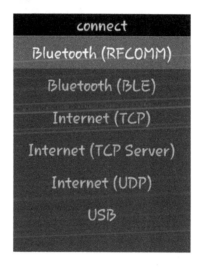

Figure3

Stage 3:- After associating with the HC-06 bluetooth module return to figure2 window and afterward click on 'alter ui' for making the UI as per your need.

At the point when snap on 'alter ui' you will again observe the window appeared in figure1 then click anyplace on the screen you will see the application window like figure4 and the select 'Catch' to get the catch structure.

Figure4

Stage 4:- After choosing the catch you will get a catch structure on the screen to alter. You can resize and move the structure anyplace on the screen. Presently, for setting the incentive to be sent on snap through Bluetooth you have 'set press activity' (as appeared in figure6) and type the worth you need to send from that specific catch. Like, we are sending '1' for pivoting the servo by squeezing the 'Start' catch in Roboremo android application.

You can check every qualities, being sent on tapping on various catches, in the table given later area.

Arduino space race game, Bluetooth, Door Lock, Voice control

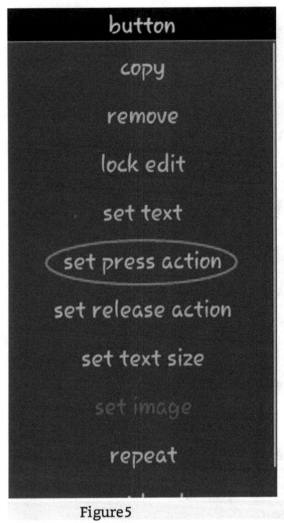

Figure 5   Figure 6

Stage 5:- Finally we have User Interface to control the servo engine utilizing Smartphone.

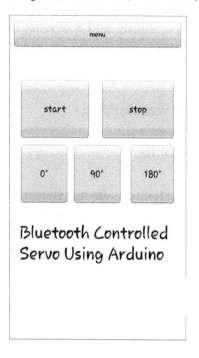

Figure 7

Code and Explanation

The total Arduino code for controlling servo engine utilizing Bluetooth is given toward the end.

Arduino has library for Servo Motors as well as it handles all the PWM related things to turn the servo, you simply have to enter the point to which you need to pivot and there is work servo1.write(angle); which will turn the servo to wanted edge.

So here we are beginning by characterizing the

library for Servo engine and Software Serial library is utilized for characterizing the Rx and Tx stick.

```
#include <SoftwareSerial.h>

#include <Servo.h>
```

In the underneath code, we are instating the Arduino pins for Rx and Tx, characterizing factors for servo and different things.

```
Servo myServo;

int TxD = 11;

int RxD = 10;

int servoposition;

int servopos;

int new1;

SoftwareSerial bluetooth(TxD, RxD);
```

Presently, arrangement all the variable and parts to beginning stage. Here we have joined the servo at ninth stick of the Arduino and made the underlying situation of servo to 0 degree. Baud rate for sequential and Bluetooth correspondence has likewise been set to 9600.

```
void setup() {

  int pos=0;

  myServo.attach(9);

  myServo.write(0);

  Serial.begin(9600);    // start serial communication at 9600bps

  bluetooth.begin(9600);

}
```

In void circle work, Arduino will check the approaching qualities constantly and turn the servo as per got an incentive from Smart telephone. Every qualities will be gotten utilizing Serial Communication.

In the event that the worth is 0 the servo will pivot to 0 degree. So also on the off chance that we send 45, 90, 135 and 180 from the Bluetooth application, the servo will pivot to 45, 90, 135 and 180 degree edge individually.

```
void loop() {

if (bluetooth.available()){

   String value = bluetooth.readString();

   servoposition = value.toInt();

   if (value.toInt() == 0){

    Serial.println(servoposition);

   myServo.write(0);

    }

    if (value.toInt() == 45){

    Serial.println(servoposition);

   myServo.write(45);

    }

    if (value.toInt() == 90){

    Serial.println(servoposition);
```

```
myServo.write(90);

}

if (value.toInt() == 135){

Serial.println(servoposition);

myServo.write(135);

}

if (value.toInt() == 180){

Serial.println(servoposition);

myServo.write(180);

}
```

In the event that we send the worth '1' by squeezing Start catch then servo will pivot constantly until stop catch is squeezed. Here we are sending '2' on squeezing stop catch, which will be perused by the Arduino and it will break the while circle and servo will be halted.

```
while(value.toInt()==1){
```

```
if (bluetooth.available())

{

value = bluetooth.readString();

Serial.println(value);

if (value.toInt()==2)

{Serial.println("YYY"); break; }

}

servopos++;

delay(30);

Serial.println(servopos);

myServo.write(servopos);

if (servopos ==180 )

{servopos=0;break;}

}

}
```

```
}
```

Working of Servo motor Control using Bluetooth:

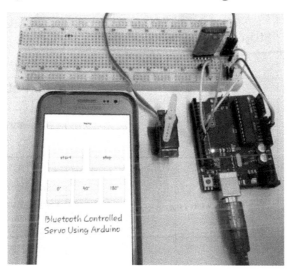

In this undertaking, we are controlling the Servo Motor utilizing an Android application "Roboremo". In this present application's interface, we have made 5 catches to control the Servo engine as clarified before. The working of each catch is given in the beneath table:

S.No.	Button Name	Sending Value	Description
1.	Start	1	This button is used to start

			rotating the servo from 0^0 to 180^0.
2.	Stop	2	This button is used to stop the servo at any point.
3.	0^0	0	This button is used to rotate the servo to 0^0.
4.	90^0	90	This button is used to rotate the servo to 90^0.
5.	180^0	180	This button is used to rotate the servo to 180^0.

Thus, by squeezing these catches on your Android application Roboremo, the information will be sent through the cell phone's Bluetooth to HC-06 Bluetooth module. From that HC-06 module information is gotten by the Arduino and Arduino turns the Servo at the point characterized in the code for the specific catch. We have additionally coded for point 45 and 135, yet because of the confinement of Roboremo application, you can just make 5 catches, so we avoided two catches.

So this is the means by which you can send the information from Smartphone to the Arduino utilizing Bluetooth to control the servo remotely. This can be utilized in numerous applications like Toy autos, robots and so on.

Code

```
#include <SoftwareSerial.h>
#include <Servo.h>
Servo myServo;
int TxD = 11;
int RxD = 10;
int servoposition;
int servopos;
int new1;
SoftwareSerial bluetooth(TxD, RxD);
void setup() {
 int pos=0;
 myServo.attach(9);
 myServo.write(0);
 Serial.begin(9600);    // start serial communication
at 9600bps
 bluetooth.begin(9600);
}
void loop() {
 if(bluetooth.available())
  {
   String value = bluetooth.readString();
   servoposition = value.toInt();
```

```
  if(value.toInt() == 0)
 {
 Serial.println(servoposition);
 myServo.write(0);
 }

   if(value.toInt() == 45)
 {
 Serial.println(servoposition);
 myServo.write(45);
 }

   if(value.toInt() == 90)
 {
 Serial.println(servoposition);
 myServo.write(90);
 }

   if(value.toInt() == 135)
 {
 Serial.println(servoposition);
 myServo.write(135);
 }

   if(value.toInt() == 180)
 {
 Serial.println(servoposition);
 myServo.write(180);
 }


  while(value.toInt()==1){
 if(bluetooth.available())
 {
```

```
value = bluetooth.readString();
Serial.println(value);
if(value.toInt()==2)
{Serial.println("YYY"); break;}


  }


  servopos++;
delay(30);
Serial.println(servopos);
myServo.write(servopos);




  if(servopos ==180)
{servopos=0;break;}



 }
 }
}
```

9.CONTROLLING MULTIPLE SERVO MOTORS WITH ARDUINO

Utilizing a couple of Servo with Arduino is Easy yet imagine a scenario where we need to utilize many Servo Motors.

Here, we are demonstrating that how to manage Multiple Servo Motors with Arduino. Interfacing numerous Servo Motors with Arduino is by all accounts simple and however on the off chance that we associate every one of the Servos to Arduino supply pins, at that point they won't work effectively in view of absence of enough current to drive every one of the engines. So you need to utilize separate power supply for the engines, possibly it be from certain connectors (5v 2A) or from great quality 9v batteries.

Material Required

- Arduino UNO
- Servo Motor
- Power Supply
- Breadboard
- Connecting Wires

Circuit Diagram

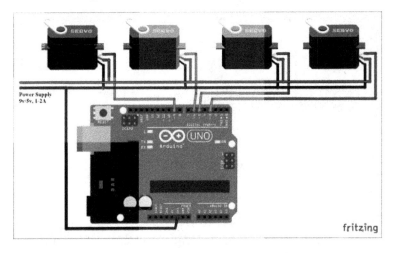

What is a Servo Motor?

Prior to really expounding, first we should think about Servo Motors.

Servo engines are accessible at various shapes and sizes. A servo engine will have basically there wires, one is for positive voltage another is for ground and last one is for position setting. The RED wire is associated with power, Black wire is associated with ground and YELLOW wire is associated with sign.

A servo engine is a blend of DC engine, position control framework, gears. The situation of the pole of the DC engine is balanced by the control gadgets in the servo, in light of the obligation proportion of the PWM signal the SIGNAL stick.

Just talking the control gadgets modify shaft position by controlling DC engine. This information with respect to position of shaft is sent through the SIGNAL stick. The position information to the control ought to be sent as PWM signal through the Signal stick of servo engine.

The recurrence of PWM (Pulse Width Modulated) sign can change dependent on kind of servo engine. The significant thing here is the DUTY RATIO of the PWM signal. In view of this DUTY RATION the control hardware alter the pole.

As appeared in figure underneath, for the pole to be moved to 9o clock the TURN ON RATION must be 1/18.ie. 1ms of ON schedule and 17ms of OFF time in a 18ms sign.

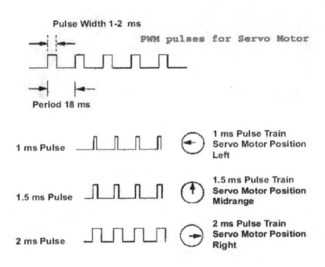

For the pole to be moved to 12o clock the ON time of sign must be 1.5ms and OFF time ought to be 16.5ms. This proportion is decoded by control framework in servo and it changes the position dependent on it.

This PWM in here is produced by utilizing ARDUINO UNO.

Before Connecting Servos to Arduino, you can check your servo with the assistance of this Servo Motor Tester Circuit. Additionally check our beneath Servo activities:

- Servo Motor Control utilizing Arduino

- Servo Motor Control with Arduino Due

- Servo Motor Interfacing with 8051 Micro-controller

- Servo Motor Control utilizing MATLAB

- Servo Motor Control by Flex Sensor

- Servo Position Control with Weight (Force Sensor)

Arduino Code Explanation

The total Arduino code for Multiple Servo Control is given toward the end.

Arduino has library for Servo Motors as well as it handles all the PWM related things to turn the servo, you simply have to enter the edge to which you need to pivot and there is work servo1.write(angle); which will turn the servo to wanted edge.

So here we are beginning by characterizing the library for Servo engine.

```
#include <Servo.h>
```

In underneath code, we are introducing all the four servos as Servo1, Servo2, Servo3, as well as Servo4.

```
Servo servo1;

Servo servo2;

Servo servo3;

Servo servo4;
```

At that point, we are setting all the servo's information stick with Arduino. As appeared in the underneath code, Servo1 is associated with the third stick of the Arduino. You can change the pins as per you however remember that it ought to be a PWM stick. Utilizing a Servo with computerized pins of the Arduino isn't dependable.

```
void setup() {

  servo1.attach(3);
```

```
    servo2.attach(5);

    servo3.attach(6);

    servo4.attach(9);

}
```

Presently, in the void circle() work we are simply pivoting all the servo from 0 to 180 degree as well as after that 180 to 0 degree. The postpone utilized in the underneath code is utilized to increment or reduction the speed of the servo as it impact the expanding or diminishing pace of variable 'I'.

```
void loop() {

  for (int i = 0; i < 180; i++) {

    servo1.write(i);

    servo2.write(i);

    servo3.write(i);

    servo4.write(i);

    delay(10);
```

```
  }

  for (i = 180; i > 0; i--) {

    servo1.write(i);

    servo2.write(i);

    servo3.write(i);

    servo4.write(i);

    delay(10);

  }

}
```

Controlling Multiple Servos with Arduino- Working:

We as a whole face current issue while utilizing multiple servos with one Arduino. The main answer for this is to interface an outside power supply with fitting measure of current rating (in this undertaking I utilized 2A with 9v supply). For External Power supply you can utilize Adapters, RPS (Regulated Power Supply Instrument) or great quality 9v volt batteries, evne you can utilize your workstation USB port for driving little Servo. To utilize the outside stockpile you simply need to short the Arduino ground to outer inventory ground.

Utilize the Arduino code offered underneath to program your Arduino and associate all the Servo Motors as appeared in the circuit outline with appropriate power supply to Motors. In this manner, all servos will cooperate with no interfere.

Code

```
#include <Servo.h>
Servo servo1;
```

```
Servo servo2;
Servo servo3;
Servo servo4;
int i = 0;
void setup() {
 servo1.attach(3);
 servo2.attach(5);
 servo3.attach(6);
 servo4.attach(9);
}
void loop() {
 for (i = 0; i < 180; i++) {
  servo1.write(i);
  servo2.write(i);
  servo3.write(i);
  servo4.write(i);
  delay(10);
 }
 for (i = 180; i > 0; i--) {
  servo1.write(i);
  servo2.write(i);
  servo3.write(i);
  servo4.write(i);
  delay(10);
 }
}
```

10.INTERFACING ARDUINO WITH MATLAB - BLINKING LED

In this undertaking, we will learn,

- The most effective method to set up equipment support for Arduino in MATLAB programming.

- Stage by stage instructions to control an Arduino utilizing MATLAB code.

We regularly use Arduino IDE to compose and transfer codes to Arduino. The upside of MATLAB is, it utilizes an abnormal state programming language which is simpler than C/C++. The other bit of leeway of utilizing MATLAB is, we can see the aftereffects of I/O activities rapidly (without assembling). In addition, MATLAB gives plotting capacities that we can use to rapidly dissect and picture information gathered from Arduino. To start with, we will figure out how to arrangement equipment bolster bundle for Arduino in MATLAB programming. In the wake of setting up equipment bolster bundle for Arduino in MATLAB programming, we are gonna to control LEDs that are associated with Arduino board utilizing MATLAB code.

Setup Hardware Support Package for MATLAB:

Stage 1. Start MATLAB (most recent Version liked).

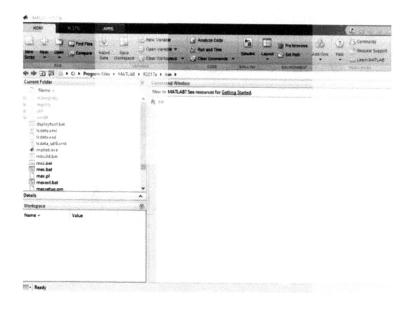

Stage 2. In the Environment segment, select Add-Ons > Get Hardware Support Packages.

Stage 3. It will begin the Add-On pioneer window.

Stage 4. Snap on MATLAB Support Package for Arduino Hardware.

Stage 5. Snap on Install, presently the installer will

request that you sign into your MathWorks account. In the event that you don't have MathWorks account, you can make a record during establishment.

Stage 6. Subsequent to signing in, Accept the permit understanding and continue to establishment.

Stage 7. Presently, trust that the bundle will download and introduce.

Stage 8. Presently you have effectively introduced Arduino Support Package for MATLAB.

Testing MATLAB:

In the wake of introducing the help bundle for MATLAB, we have to check whether it is introduced appropriately or not.

1. Open MATLAB.

2. Associate Arduino to PC.

3. Type the accompanying direction in MATLAB order window.

```
a = arduino()
```

4. On the off chance that we have more than one Arduino associated with PC, at that point we can determine the board type and COM port to which it is associated utilizing the accompanying order.

> **a = arduino('COM5' , 'uno')**

5. Subsequent to entering the above direction, MATLAB will attempt to speak with your Arduino, if fruitful, MATLAB will show the properties of Arduino board associated with PC.

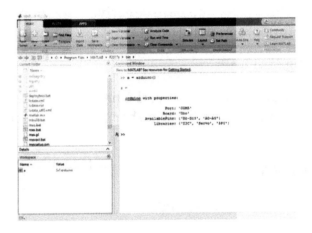

6. Presently we can see the variable 'an' in the workspace, which is the MATLAB arduino object. To clear the article we can use the accompanying order.

> **clear a**

It will expel the Arduino object from the workspace.

Controlling LEDs using MATLAB and Arduino:

In this model, we are going to squint a LED that is associated with Arduino utilizing MATLAB.

Components Required:

- Arduino
- LEDs
- Resistors
- USB link for Arduino

Schematic:

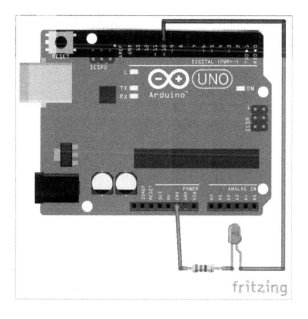

Steps:

1. Start MATLAB.

2. Associate your Arduino to PC.

3. Make the circuit as appeared in the schematic.

4. Open your .m code.

5. Spare it and Run.

6. Driven beginnings Blinking.

7. Subsequent to flickering multiple times, LED turns off.

Code is extremely straightforward and it is given beneath, duplicate it and spare it in document with .m expansion. You can play around the code and tweak it as indicated by your necessities.

Further in the event that you need become familiar with MATLAB graphical Interface with Arduino check this venture: GUI Based Home Automation System utilizing Arduino and MATLAB

Code

% create an arduino object

```
a = arduino();
% start the loop to blink led for 5 seconds
for i = 1:5
    writeDigitalPin(a, 'D10', 1);
    pause(0.5);
    writeDigitalPin(a, 'D10', 0);
    pause(0.5);
end
% end communication with arduino
clear a
```

Thank you !!!